Butterfly Fields

A Scrap Quilter's Journey

By Carolyn Nixon
and Betsey Langford

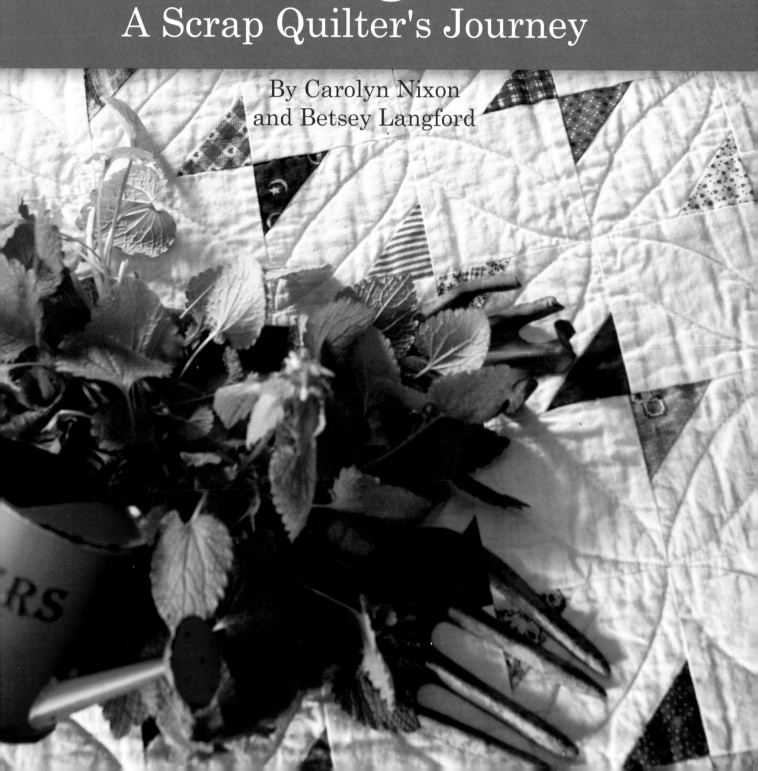

Butterfly Fields:
A Scrap Quilter's Journey

Editor: Donna di Natale
Designer: Kelly Ludwig
Photography: Aaron T. Leimkuehler
Illustration: Eric Sears
Technical Editor: Christina DeArmond
Production Assistant: Jo Ann Groves

Published by:
Kansas City Star Books
1729 Grand Blvd.
Kansas City, Missouri, USA 64108
All rights reserved
Copyright © 2013 Carolyn Nixon, Betsey
Langford and The Kansas City Star Co.

First edition, first printing
ISBN: 978-1-61169-086-6
Library of Congress Control Number:
2013933478

Printed in the United States of America by
Walsworth Publishing Co., Marceline, MO
To order copies, call StarInfo at
(816) 234-4242.

www.PickleDish.com

Kansas City Star Quilts

Dedication

I dedicate *Butterfly Fields* in loving memory to my mother, Pearl Brown. My heart knows that she is still there somewhere, smiling as she sits among the fragrant flowers of a garden filled with butterflies.

Carolyn Nixon

I dedicate *Butterfly Fields* to my precious daughters, Emily and Sara, who fill my life with butterfly kisses. You are my joy and inspiration.

Betsey Langford

Butterfly Fields

Table of Contents

Hairstreak on Chives
Photo by Patrick di Natale

About the Authors

Carolyn Nixon

A public school educator for the past 32 years, I currently work as an instructional coach for Willard R-II School District in Willard, Missouri. The perfect end to any day is sitting at my sewing machine working on a quilting project. Actually, I cannot remember a time without the comfort of handmade quilts. As a young child, my mother let me stand beside her and help as she tacked and hand-tied quilts on her quilting frame. In the summer of my eighth year I learned to knit, crochet, tat, smock and use fabric paint. I remember painting giant pink roses on a white sheet and crocheting pink lace edging to make a bed cover. Garment sewing followed soon after. Although quilting was part of my mother's everyday life, it wasn't until near the age of 40 that I got hooked. Once bitten, forever gone! The icing on my cake is having the opportunity to share my passion for quilting with others. Enjoy!

Betsey Langford

My quilting journey began at the age of 18 when I learned how to hand piece and quilt. It was a joyful experience and I took to it like a duck to water. After mastering the art and technique of hand-quilting, it seemed natural to begin creating my own designs. Desiring to share my passion for quilting with others, I began teaching handquilting classes at a local quilt shop. Eventually, I opened my own shop in Bolivar, Missouri. During the years as a shop owner, it was a privilege to share my quilting and design work with faithful customers who frequented the shop. In my current position as education director for Gammill Quilting Systems, I continue to share my love of quilting with others.

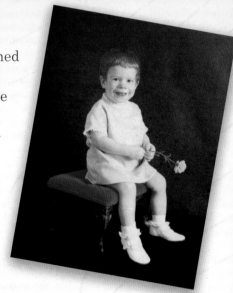

Acknowledgements

Doug Weaver and Diane McLendon. A special thanks to you for believing in us and giving us the opportunity to do another book with Kansas City Star Quilts.

Donna di Natale. We loved working with you as our editor. Your vivacious and caring spirit made this a joyful and memorable adventure. From beginning to end, you were a sensational, attentive team leader, totally in tune with our vision for *Butterfly Fields*. Thank you for bringing our work to life in superlative fashion.

Mark and Dixie Dawson, innkeepers at Blackberry Creek Bed & Breakfast and Retreat in Rogersville, MO. From the very beginning of this project, it was certain that your beautiful bed and breakfast home was the perfect place to do the photo shoot for Butterfly Fields. We are thankful for your gracious hospitality and faithful support of our passion for the art of quilting.

Christina DeArmond. Thanks for your attention to detail in checking the accuracy of our sewing instructions and for correctly counting all the pieces.

Kelly Ludwig. Thank you for capturing the essence of our designs and pulling it all together into a beautiful book.

Eric Sears. Thanks for your talent and attention to detail on pattern templates and illustrations.

Aaron Leimkuehler. It was a pleasure to work with you again, Aaron. Your eye for detail and careful consideration of color, shape and balance is evident in the dazzling photographs of *Butterfly Fields*.

Edie McGinnis. It was also a pleasure to meet and work with you again, Edie. We appreciate your willingness to make the long trek to Rogersville to provide guidance and assistance with the photo shoot. Your entertaining luncheon story about an infamous ovine and feline duo will long be remembered by Carolyn and her daughter Laura.

Jo Ann Groves. Thank you, Jo Ann, for your preparation of the photographs for the designer. We appreciate the time you spent to precisely match all the colors of the original projects.

Betsy Betros. Please accept our heartfelt appreciation for allowing us access to the beautiful photography of *A Photographic Field Guide to the Butterflies in the Kansas City Region*.

Laura Walker. Special appreciation is extended to Laura Walker, Carolyn's daughter. Thank you for taking time out of your busy schedule to spend the day helping with the photo shoot at Blackberry Creek.

Patrick di Natale. Thanks for the lovely butterfly and wildflower photos that add so much to the book, and for your assistance with the photo shoot.

Michelle Ashley, Barbara Stephens, Lindsay Lawing & Lisa Sipes. Ladies, we love the unveiling — those moments when quilts come back and our breaths are taken away by the magic of your quilting. Thank you for being part of our quilting legacy.

Nancy Jones. Thanks for letting us use your quilt to photograph the larger-size version of the Butterfly Fields quilt.

Genny Nasse. A special note of thanks from Carolyn. I thank you for all the bits and pieces of fabric you passed my way as I was making Butterfly Fields. I treasure your friendship.

Our Families. Your undying love and support for our quilting habits does not go unnoticed.

Thanks for overlooking the sewing machine on the sun porch, the cutting mat on the kitchen table, the basket of scraps in the middle of the living room floor, and for all the other unlikely and often unpredictable places where our love of quilting and quilting friends overflow into your lives. We cut and sew fabric together because we love it; we love you; we want to pass it on.

Designed and Created
by Carolyn Nixon
For Blackberry Creek Bed
& Breakfast and Retreat

Welcome to Butterfly Fields

Metamorphosis is a good term to describe the journey that ends with this book. It began in January of 2002 when my mother died. Although she was 91 years old and ready to leave this earth, it was a time of great sadness for me. In the weeks following her passing, I retreated into silence and spun myself up in a cocoon of grief and loss. Turning to my sewing machine for solace, I sought to preserve Mama's memory in unbleached muslin and scrap pieces of fabric. Eventually, black fabric took the place of the muslin, but the scraps remained my constant companion for many months. Feasting on fabric day after day, I created a few blocks at a time. Eventually, a wellspring of new life began to bubble through my veins. I shed the cocoon and went back to life with a peaceful heart and two personal treasures, Butterfly Fields and Mama's Black Pearls.

Life continued, and several years later Betsey and I became owners of Quilted Heart, a quilt shop located in Bolivar, Missouri. Brimming with enthusiasm and ideas, we were creating our own designs for quilts and projects. Betsey used her drafting talents to create patterns for Butterfly Fields and Mama's Black Pearls. Inspired, I started experimenting with inserting 3-dimensional folded blocks (butterflies) into traditional block patterns. Butterfly Log Cabin and Butterfly Goes A-Courtin' were born from those efforts. Meanwhile, Betsey was busy designing Butterfly Star, Butterfly Comes to Dinner and Butterfly Garden. We created Butterfly Button Boodle, Butterfly Journey Table Runner, Butterfly Star Framed Block and Butterfly Hand Towels to satisfy the taste of those preferring smaller quilting projects.

But the story goes on … an amazing butterfly journey! Betsey and I now have the great joy of sharing our ideas with you via this lovely quilt book. Now it is your turn. May the soft whisper of butterfly wings caress your soul and quiet your spirit. We wish you many hours of sewing pleasure filled with beautiful fabric and peaceful contemplation.

Carolyn

Monarch Butterfly, Photo
by Patrick di Natale

Butterfly Tidbits and Garden Tips

*E*njoy your time here in *Butterfly Fields*. Relax and imagine yourself on a quiet, peaceful day, strolling along a cobblestone pathway in some hidden garden far from all the cares of the world. As you journey along, be on the lookout for butterflies. Revel in the beauty of these gorgeous, winged creatures. As you journey through this book, you will find tips and tidbits of interesting information. For those of you with a bit of soil and a desire to plant, there are tips for creating your very own butterfly garden. In order to sustain the life cycle of caterpillars and butterflies in your garden realm, pay close attention to the butterfly nectar and caterpillar cuisine notes for each species of butterfly.

Sources

Each project is accompanied by a Garden Invitation to assist in inviting butterflies to your yard. The invitation includes a butterfly photo, common name and species; the time of the year during which the butterfly is seen in the Midwest; the nectar that the caterpillar thrives on; and the cuisine preferred by the butterfly. The butterflies associated with the invitations are common to the Kansas City region, but are also found in many areas around the nation. *A Photographic Field Guide to the Butterflies in the Kansas City Region*, authored by Betsy Betros and published by Kansas City Star Books, was the source of the photos and much of the information given. Additional information was collected from online resources.

Many of the varieties recommended for caterpillar cuisine and butterfly nectar are available from the Missouri Wildflowers Nursery, located just south of Jefferson City, Missouri. Mervin Wallace is the mastermind behind the nursery; he has been harvesting and selling the seeds of native perennials since 1984. When asked why native wildflowers, Mervin stated, "I am supplying native plants that are as 'wild' as I can produce them, because I feel it is a way to help native species continue their journey through time. May each species live long and prosper."

For those who would like to visit Missouri Wildflower Nursery, business hours and a map are available on the nursery website (*http://www.mowildflowers.net*). The site also has a selection guide, pricing, growing information, and an extensive photo gallery that showcases a host of native Missouri wildflowers.

Butterfly Garden Tips

▷ Butterfly weed, purple coneflowers and New England asters are the three most popular nectar producing plant foods for butterflies. In addition, these lovely creatures enjoy the nectar of milkweed, marigolds, oregano, and butterfly bush. The best strategy for attracting many different butterflies is to plant a variety of flowers in your garden.

▷ It is a good idea to create groupings of flowers that are alike. Butterflies that have an appetite for a certain variety can feast within a small area of your garden.

▷ Paying careful attention to the blooming season of garden plants ensures that there will be a succession of blooms to provide food for butterflies. This extends the season of time for enjoying their presence.

▷ Butterflies are unable to fly when their body temperature falls below 86°. When temperatures are chilly, strategically placed flat rocks or paver stones can help. The stones absorb heat and provide a place for butterflies to bask or warm themselves. In the cooler morning hours, you might catch a glimpse of one perching on a stone, usually with its wings held above its body or straight out to the side. When warm enough, it will take flight and begin to flit about from flower to flower in search of nectar.

▷ Butterflies need water sources. A shallow birdbath works great. Surprisingly, most butterflies actually prefer to drink from a mud puddle or sand pool that provides moisture as well as needed minerals. A simple method for creating a water source is to dig into the soil, place a shallow pan or dish, fill it with sand or dirt and add some water. Be sure to check the spot each day; provide enough water to keep it moist and inviting for your winged friends.

▷ Two types of plants are needed for hosting the entire life cycle of butterflies. Nectar plants are necessary to supply food for adult butterflies, and caterpillar food plants are needed to feed caterpillars.

▷ Well-placed shrubs about the perimeter of a garden can help protect butterflies from the wind, thus making it easier for butterflies to explore. They also provide a place to roost at night, as well as a place to hide from predators.

▷ Butterflies prefer temperatures that range from 85° to 100° Fahrenheit. Make your guests happy by locating your garden where there is direct sunlight for at least six to eight hours per day.

Butterfly Tidbits

▷ A rare butterfly from the rain forest of New Guinea is the largest known species of butterfly; the Queen Alexandra Birdwing (*Ornithoptera alexandrae*) has a 12" wingspan.

▷ The Western Pygmy Blue butterfly (*Brephidium exilis*), the smallest of all butterflies, is slightly over a half inch in length.

▷ To check to see if a leaf will be good caterpillar food, many types of butterflies taste with their feet. If the leaf is good caterpillar cuisine, eggs can be laid on the spot.

▷ Butterflies have an outer exoskeleton that keeps water inside their bodies and helps to protect them.

▷ The beautiful source of color on butterflies is their scales which are layered like shingles on a rooftop; these are hollow, air-filled areas which serve as insulation and help make the creatures more aerodynamic.

▷ Because butterflies are sensitive to movement and have amazing vision, one has to be quite sneaky to capture them on film. It is thought that their faceted, compound eyes can see all colors of the light spectrum plus ultraviolet and infrared light.

▷ Butterflies feed through a sucking device called a proboscis, a tube that is kept coiled under the head when not in use.

▷ Butterflies breathe through holes located on the abdomen. These holes, called spiracles, are used to transfer oxygen into the body and carbon dioxide out.

▷ Butterflies have four wings that are used to attract the opposite sex, for flight and for protection from predators.

▷ During courtship, both female and male butterflies emit pheromones from scent patches on their wings. The process is called "dusting" and the purpose is to stimulate mating.

Buckeye Butterfly, photo
by Patrick di Natale

Spicebush Swallowtail
Photo by Betsy Betros

Garden Invitation

The Spicebush Swallowtail *Papilio troilus*
March to October

Butterfly Nectar

Spicebush, Bergamot, Sweet William & Butterfly Bush

Caterpillar Cuisine

Sassafras & Spicebush

Butterfly Fields

PIECED BY CAROLYN NIXON
QUILTED BY MICHELLE ASHLEY

I see before me a never-ending kaleidoscope, wing upon wing, a priceless portrait created by the hand of God. Mere words cannot express such a vision of glory. With loving care, bits of fabric become the messengers. In my mind and heart, each butterfly represents a loving memory of Mama; united, they come as a swarm of butterflies in flight across a wildflower meadow. When all of life is said and done, memories — like the soft whisper of butterfly wings — remain.

~Journal Entry, Carolyn Nixon, 2002

Fabric Requirements

Butterfly Fields can be made with little 3″ butterfly blocks or larger 5″ butterfly blocks, depending on your preference. The quilt in the photo on page 12 was made with 3″ blocks; the quilt in the photo on page 17 was made with 5″ blocks. Select a block size and quilt size and follow the appropriate yardage and cutting instructions.

3″ Blocks	Throw	Twin	Full	Queen
Finished Size	60″ x 60″	60″ x 84″	78″ x 90″	84″ x 96″
	400 blocks	560 blocks	780 blocks	896 blocks
Background Fabric	4 yards	5 yards	7 yards	8 yards
Scrap Fabric	1 ¼ yard	1 ¾ yards	2 ¼ yards	2 ¾ yards

5″ Blocks	Throw	Twin	Full	Queen
Finished Size	60″ x 70″	60″ x 80″	80″ x 90″	90″ x 100″
	168 blocks	192 blocks	288 blocks	360 blocks
Background Fabric	4 yards	5 yards	6 ½ yards	8 yards
Scrap Fabric	1 ¼ yard	1 ½ yards	1 ⅞ yards	2 ¼ yards

Cutting Instructions

3″ blocks	Quilt Size	Finished Size	Background Fabric	Scrap Fabric
	Throw	60″ x 60″	400 – 3 ½″ Squares	400 – 2″ Squares
	Twin	60″ x 84″	560 – 3 ½″ Squares	560 – 2″ Squares
	Full	78″ x 90″	780 – 3 ½″ Squares	780 – 2″ Squares
	Queen	84″ x 96″	896 – 3 ½″ Squares	896 – 2″ Squares

5″ blocks	Quilt Size	Finished Size	Background Fabric	Scrap Fabric
	Throw	60″ x 70″	168 – 5 ½″ Squares	168 – 3″ Squares
	Twin	60″ x 80″	192 – 5 ½″ Squares	192 – 3″ Squares
	Full	80″ x 90″	288 – 5 ½″ Squares	288 – 3″ Squares
	Queen	90″ x 100″	360 – 5 ½″ Squares	360 – 3″ Squares

The Butterfly Block

1. Prepare the scrap squares by drawing a line from corner to corner diagonally across the square on the reverse side of the fabric.

2. Set aside half of the background blocks to use as alternate blocks.

3. Lay a scrap square on the bottom left corner of the background square, right sides together. Be sure the edges of the scrap square align evenly with the background fabric before sewing.

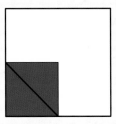

4. Sew on the drawn line.

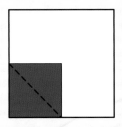

5. Flip the scrap square up to be sure it is even. Trim, leaving a ¼″ seam allowance. Press the seam allowance toward the scrap.

6. Repeat on the opposite background corner.

7. Make enough Butterfly Blocks to use half of the background squares.

Quilt Assembly

Sew each Butterfly Block to an alternate block (the background squares set aside at the beginning) to make rows. See the chart on page 17 for how many blocks to put in each row.

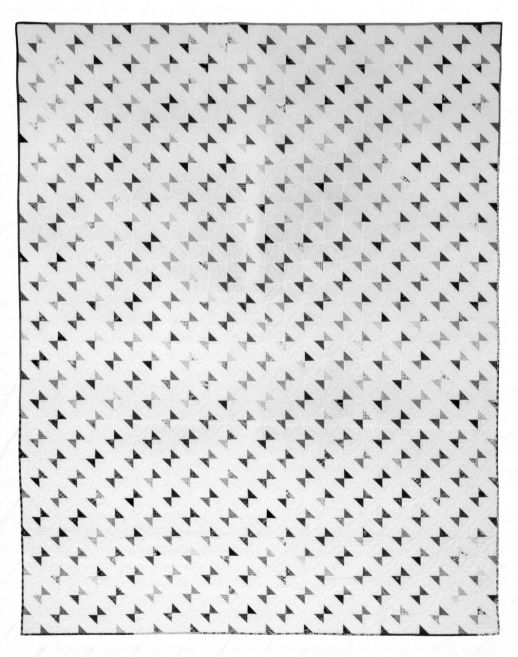

Referring to the photograph below, sew the rows together, alternating the rows so that every other row begins with a Butterfly Block.

Quilt and bind.

Block Guide

Butterfly Fields using 3″ Blocks:

Throw	60″ x 60″	20 blocks by 20 blocks
Twin	60″ x 84″	20 blocks by 28 blocks
Full	78″ x 90″	26 blocks by 30 blocks
Queen	84″ x 96″	28 blocks by 32 blocks

Butterfly Fields using 5″ blocks:

Throw	60″ x 70″	12 blocks by 14 blocks
Twin	60″ x 80″	12 blocks by 16 blocks
Full	80″ x 90″	16 blocks by 18 blocks
Queen	90″ x 100″	18 blocks by 20 blocks

*"We are like butterflies who flutter for a day
and think it is forever." — Carl Sagan*

Garden Invitation

Clouded Sulphur *Colias philodice*
March to December

Butterfly Nectar

Sweet Clover, Milkvetch & Alfalfa

Caterpillar Cuisine

Tall Thoroughwort

Clouded Sulphur
Photo by Betsy Betros

Butterfly Journey Table Runner

PIECED BY CAROLYN NIXON
QUILTED BY CAROLYN NIXON
FINISHED SIZE: 20˝ X 44˝

*O*ne of life's simple pleasures is to spend a lazy summer afternoon sitting in a flower-filled garden, reading a book and sipping ice-cold lemonade. Time seems to stand still momentarily as one pauses to observe the silent flight of butterflies, flitting from flower to flower in search of nectar. Capture the flight path of butterflies in fabric and stitches; let the work of your hands be a constant reminder of peaceful summer days in the sunshine.

Fabric Requirements

- Background: ⅝ yard
- Outer Border and Binding: 1 yard
- Butterflies: ¼ yard
- Inner Border: ⅛ yard
- Backing: 1 ½ yard

Cutting Instructions

For the background, cut:

- 10 – 4 ½″ white muslin squares
- 8 – 2 ½″ x 4 ½″ white muslin rectangles
- 52 – 2 ½″ white muslin squares

For the butterflies, cut:

- 26 – 2″ red print squares

For the Inner Border, cut:

- 2 – 1 ½″ x 12 ½″ red print strips
- 2 – 1 ½″ x 38 ½″ red print strips

For the Outer Border, cut:

- 2 – 3 ½″ x 14 ½″ white muslin strips
- 3 – 3 ½″ x width of fabric white muslin strips (sew 3 strips together along the short side; from this long strip cut 2 – 3 ½″ x 44 ½″ pieces)

For the binding, cut:

- 4 – 2 ½″ x width of fabric red print strips

The Butterfly Block

1. To make a wing unit, fold a 2″ red print square in half diagonally, wrong sides together. Gently press on the fold. Place the folded square in the corner of a 2 ½″ white muslin square.

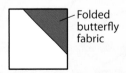

Folded butterfly fabric

2. Lay another 2 ½″ white muslin square on top, right sides together, making a sandwich. Sew along an edge with the butterfly fabric (see illustration). Stitch seams carefully being sure to keep raw edges and corners of the fabrics aligned. Make two wing units.

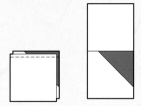

3. Position the two pieces created in step 2 so they form a butterfly unit, as illustrated below. Place right sides together and sew. Press the seams open or break the seam and press them in opposite directions. Make 13 Butterfly blocks.

Center Assembly

Sew each row using Butterfly blocks, 4 ½″ squares and 2 ½″ x 4 ½″ rectangles, according to the diagrams.

Row 1:

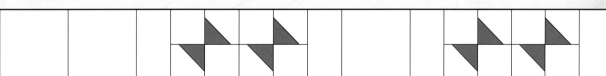

Row 2:

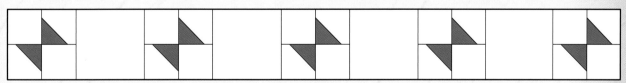

Row 3:

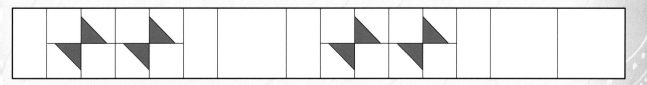

Sew the rows together.

Borders

Inner Border

1. Sew a 1 ½″ x 12 ½″ red print strip to one end of the center. Repeat for the end.
2. Sew a 1 ½″ x 38 ½″ red print strip to the side of the center. Repeat for the other side.

Outer Border

1. Sew a 3 ½″ x 14 ½″ white muslin strip to one end of the center. Repeat for the other end.
2. Sew a 3 ½″ x 44 ½″ white muslin strip to one side of the center. Repeat for the other side.
3. Quilt as desired and bind.

"May the wings of the butterfly kiss the sun
And find your shoulder to light on,
To bring you luck, happiness and riches
Today, tomorrow and beyond."
— Irish Blessing

Variegated Fritillary
Photo by Betsy Betros

Garden Invitation

The Variegated Fritillary *Euptoieta claudia*
April to November

Butterfly Nectar

Heath Aster & Pansies

Caterpillar Cuisine

Pansies, Violets Moonseed, Plantain & Passion Vine

Butterfly Cabin

FINISHED SIZE: 96˝ X 96˝
BLOCK SIZE: 12˝
PIECED BY CAROLYN NIXON
QUILTED BY BARBARA STEPHENS

*O*nce upon a time, Carolyn went out to play in her fabric garden. She folded a 3-dimensional butterfly and decided to capture it in a traditional log cabin quilt block. Before she knew what was happening, butterfly blocks multiplied and grew into a queen-size quilt. Betsey loved the idea so much that she drafted projects of every imaginable size. Carolyn and Betsey are living happily ever after and invite you to join their fairy tale by making your own Butterfly Cabin quilt.

Fabric Requirements

Background (center square):

▷ 1 ¼ yards light print

Butterfly:

▷ ½ yard red print

Four Dark Prints:

▷ ⅔ yard (A)
▷ 1 ¼ yards (B)
▷ 1 ¼ yards (C)
▷ 1 ⅔ yards (D)

Four Light Prints:

▷ 1 yard (E)
▷ 1 yard (F)
▷ 1 ½ yards (G)
▷ 1 ½ yards (H)

Binding:

▷ ¾ yard

Cutting Instructions

For Butterfly Block, cut:

▷ 256 – 2 ½″ x 2 ½″ background print squares
▷ 128 – 2″ x 2″ red print squares

For Log Cabin, cut 64 each of the following:

▷ 64 – 2 ½″ x 4 ½″ dark print A
▷ 64 – 2 ½″ x 6 ½″ light print E
▷ 64 – 2 ½″ x 6 ½″ light print F
▷ 64 – 2 ½″ x 8 ½″ dark print B
▷ 64 – 2 ½″ x 8 ½″ dark print C
▷ 64 – 2 ½″ x 10 ½″ light print G
▷ 64 – 2 ½″ x 10 ½″ light print H
▷ 64 – 2 ½″ x 12 ½″ dark print D

The Butterfly Block

1. To make a wing unit, fold a 2″ x 2″ red print square in half diagonally, wrong sides together. Gently press on the fold. Place the folded square in one corner of a 2 ½″ x 2 ½″ background print square.

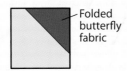
Folded butterfly fabric

2. Lay another 2 ½″ x 2 ½″ background print square on top, right sides together, making a sandwich. Sew along one edge as shown in the diagram. Stitch seams carefully being sure to keep raw edges and corners of the fabrics aligned. Make two wing units.

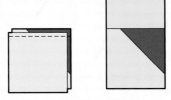

3. Flip the "wings" of the wing units so they go in opposite directions when put right sides together. Sew. Press the seams open or break the seam and press them in opposite directions.

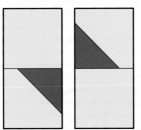 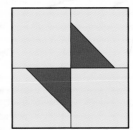

Make 64 Butterfly Blocks.

Cabin Blocks

1. 1. Sew a 2 ½″ x 4 ½″ dark print A rectangle to the butterfly block. Press seams toward the dark print.

2. Sew a 2 ½″ x 6 ½″ light print E rectangle to the unit created in step 1. Press seams toward the light print rectangle. Size to 6 ½″ square.

NOTE: It is important to check the size and trim at each step of the Cabin Block. This will insure that the block is square when completed.

3. Sew a 2 ½″ x 6 ½″ light print F rectangle to the unit created in step 2. Press seams toward the light print rectangle.

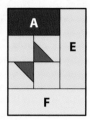

4. Sew a 2 ½″ x 8 ½″ dark print B rectangle to the unit created in step 3. Press seams toward the dark print rectangle. Size to 8 ½″ square.

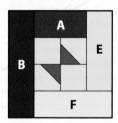

5. Sew a 2 ½″ x 8½″ dark print C rectangle to the unit created in step 4. Press seams toward the dark print rectangle.

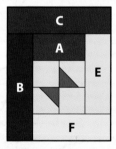

6. Sew a 2 ½″ x 10 ½″ light print G rectangle to the unit created in step 5. Press seams toward the light print rectangle. Size to 10 ½″ square.

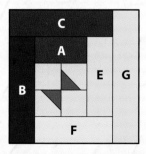

7. Sew a 2 ½″ x 10 ½″ light print H rectangle to the unit created in step 6. Press seams toward the light print rectangle.

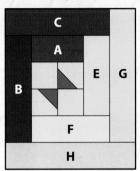

8. Sew a 2 ½″ x 12 ½″ dark print D rectangle to the unit created in step 7. Press seams toward the dark print rectangle. Size to 12 ½″ square.

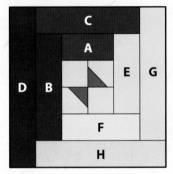

9. Repeat steps 1-7 with the remaining butterfly units to make 64 Butterfly Cabin Blocks.

Quilt Assembly

Using the assembly diagram on page 30, sew the Butterfly Cabin Blocks together into rows.

Sew the rows together to create the quilt.

Quilt as desired and bind.

"Moss covered paths between scarlet peonies,
Pale jade mountains fill your rustic windows.
I envy you, drunk with flowers,
Butterflies swirling in your dreams."
— Ch'ien Ch'i, translated by Kenneth Rexroth

Butterfly Cabin Layout Guide

Garden Invitation

The Great Spangled Fritillary Speyeria cybele
May to early October

Butterfly Nectar

Butterfly Milkweed, Purple Coneflower, & Ironweed

Caterpillar Cuisine

Passion Flower & Violets

Great Spangled Fritillary
Photo by Betsy Betros

Button Boodle

MADE BY CAROLYN NIXON

How many times have you purchased an article of clothing and ended up with an extra button or two? Carolyn's Butterfly Button Boodle to the rescue! This little jewel-of-a-project is the perfect butterfly storage closet for those extras, a charming solution when you need to replace a lost button. Simply open your Butterfly Boodle treasure chest, retrieve the necessary button, and find all the supplies needed to make your garment whole again.

Fabric Requirements:

Butterfly Cabin Block:

▷ Scrap of orange print fabric
▷ Scrap of white print fabric
▷ Scraps of four different yellow print fabrics

Backing and Lining:

▷ 1 fat quarter of green print fabric
▷ Scrap of batting
▷ Scraps from three green wools
▷ Black Perle Cotton thread

Cutting Instructions:

Butterfly Cabin block:

▷ 2 – 1″ orange print squares
▷ 4 – 1 ½″ white print squares
▷ 1 – 1 ½″ x 2 ½″ dark green print rectangle
▷ 2 – 1 ½″ x 3 ½″ yellow print rectangles from different fabrics
▷ 2 – 1 ½″ x 4 ½″ green print rectangles from different fabrics
▷ 2 – 1 ½″ x 5 ½″ yellow print rectangles from different fabrics
▷ 1 – 1 ½″ x 6 ½″ dark green print rectangle

Back & Lining:

▷ 1 – 6 ½″ green print square
▷ 1 – 6 ½″ x 12 ½″ green print rectangle
▷ 1 – 6″ x 12″ batting rectangle

Wool Pieces:

▷ 1 – 3″ x 5″ green wool rectangle
▷ 1 – 2″ light green wool square
▷ 1 – 2″ dark green wool square

Butterfly Cabin Block Assembly

Butterfly Unit

1. To make a wing unit, fold a 1″ orange print square in half diagonally, wrong sides together. Finger press the fold. Using the diagram below for placement, place the folded square in the corner of a 1 ½″ white print square.

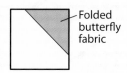
Folded butterfly fabric

2. Lay another 1 ½″ white print square on top, right sides together, making a sandwich. While keeping the raw edges and corners of the fabrics aligned, sew along one edge securing the folded butterfly square on one side. Repeat step 1 and 2 to make another wing unit.

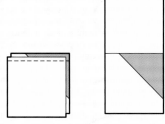

3. Flip the folded butterfly squares of the two wing units so they go in opposite directions. Place the units right sides together. Sew. Press the seams open or break the seam and press them in opposite directions. Size to 2 ½″ square.

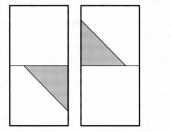 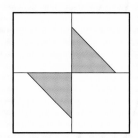

Cabin Block

1. Referring to the diagram, sew a 1 ½″ x 2 ½″ dark green print rectangle to the butterfly unit. Press seams toward the dark print.

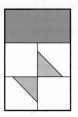

2. Referring to the diagram, sew a 1 ½″ x 3 ½″ yellow print rectangle to the unit created in step 1. Press seams toward the light print rectangle. Size to 3 ½″ square.

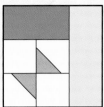

3. Referring to the diagram, sew a 1 ½″ x 3 ½″ yellow print rectangle to the unit created in step 2. Press seams toward the light print rectangle.

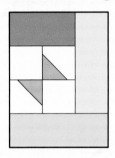

4. Referring to the diagram, sew a 1 ½″ x 4 ½″ green print rectangle to the unit created in step 3. Press seams toward the dark print rectangle. Size to 4 ½″ square.

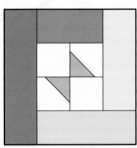

5. Referring to the diagram, sew a 1 ½″ x 4 ½″ green print rectangle to the unit created in step 4. Press seams toward the dark print rectangle.

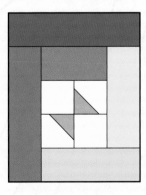

6. Referring to diagram, sew a 1 ½″ x 5 ½″ yellow print rectangle to the unit created in step 5. Press seams toward the light print rectangle. Size to 5 ½″ square.

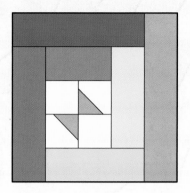

7. Referring to diagram, sew a 1 ½″ x 5 ½″ yellow print rectangle to the unit created in step 6. Press seams toward the light print rectangle.

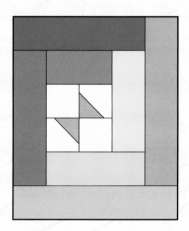

8. Referring to diagram, sew a 1 ½″ x 6 ½″ dark green rectangle to the unit created in step 7. Press seams toward the dark print rectangle to complete the butterfly unit. Size to 6 ½″ square.

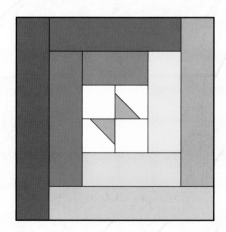

Boodle Assembly

1. Sew the 6 ½″ dark green square to the butterfly cabin unit.

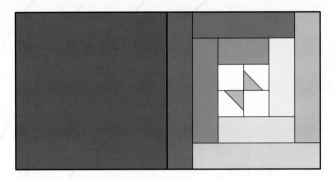

2. Measure ½″ from the bottom and left side of the 6 ½″ x 12 ½″ green lining fabric and pin the 3″ x 5″ wool green rectangle in place.

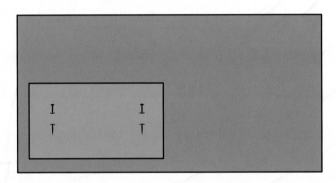

3. Using black Perle cotton thread, stitch the 3″ x 5″ wool green rectangle in place with a buttonhole stitch.

4. Measuring 1″ from the bottom and 2 ¾″ from the right hand side of the 6 ½″ x 12 ½″ green lining fabric, pin the 2″ dark green wool square in place.

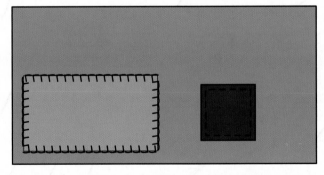

5. Using black Perle cotton thread, secure the 2″ dark green wool square in place with a running stitch.

6. Measuring ½″ from the top and ¾″ from the right side of the 6 ½″ x 12 ½″ green lining fabric, pin the 2″ light green wool square on point in place.

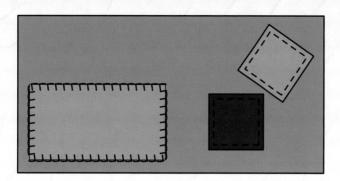

7. Using black Perle cotton thread, secure the 2″ dark green wool square in place with a running stitch.

8. Lay the 6 ½″ x 12 ½″ lining rectangle on the butterfly block cover piece, right sides together. Lay the 6″ x 12″ batting rectangle on top and pin the layers together.

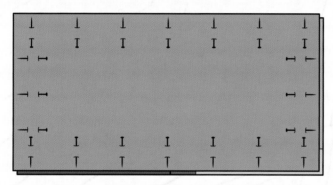

9. Sew around the edges of the boodle using a ¼″ seam allowance and leaving a 2″ opening along the bottom edge for turning.

10. Trim the corners of the boodle and turn right side out.

11. Press the edges of the boodle and slipstitch the opening shut.

12. Sew the button to the front of the boodle at the center of the open edge.

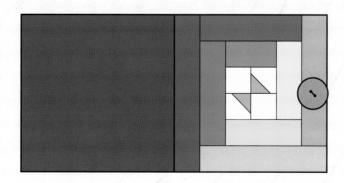

13. Using Perle cotton thread, take securing stitches on the opposite side from where the button is and tie a knot, leaving the ends 4″ long.

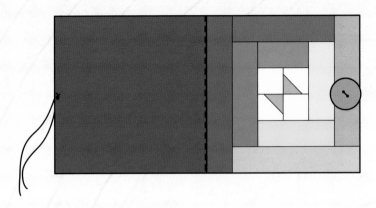

14. Using Perle cotton thread, stitch down the center fold of the boodle with a running stitch.

15. Using Perle cotton thread, take securing stitches on the left hand side, 1 ½″ from the top and 1″ from the center fold (or where you prefer to put the scissors). Tie a knot and leave the ends 6″ long.

16. Using Perle Cotton, take securing stitches on the right side 1 ½″ from the top and 1 ½″ from the center fold (or preferred for threader placement). Tie a knot and leave ends 6″ long.

Thread for scissors   Thread for needle threader

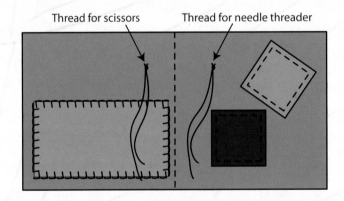

17. Tie scissors to the left hand side of the boodle and a threader to the right hand side. Use the bottom left wool panel for pins and the top right piece for needles. Load a safety pin with spare buttons and secure to the bottom right wool square.

"Beautiful and graceful, varied and enchanting, small but approachable, butterflies lead you to the sunny side of life. And everyone deserves a little sunshine." — Jefferey Glassberg

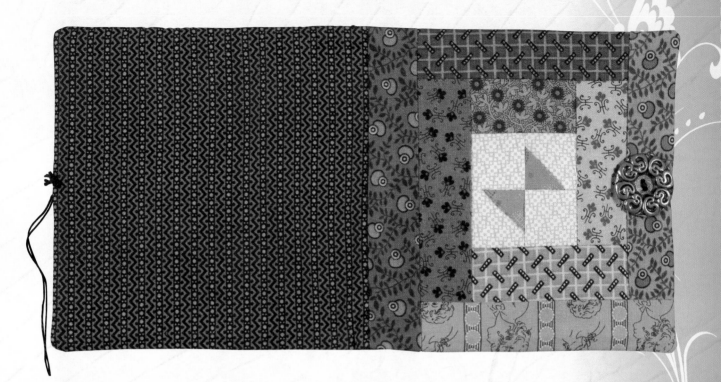

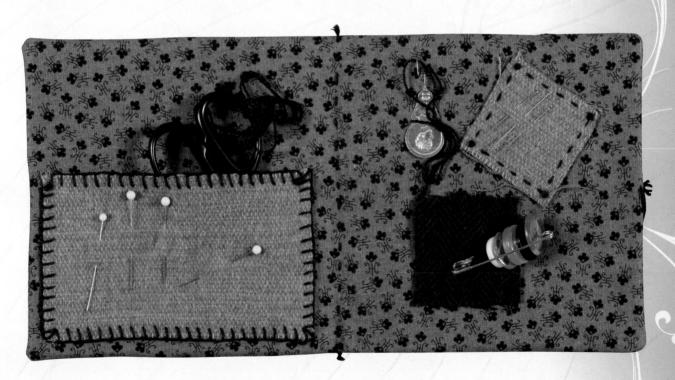

Garden Invitation

The Olive Juniper Hairstreak *Callophrys gryneus*
February to November

Butterfly Nectar

Mountain Mint, Oxeye Daisy,
Queen Anne's Lace & Whorled Milkweed

Caterpillar Cuisine

Cedar Trees

Olive Juniper Hairstreak
Photo by Betsy Betros

Butterfly Goes A-Courtin'

PIECED BY CAROLYN NIXON
QUILTED BY LINDSAY LAWING
FINISHED SIZE: 88˝ X 100˝
FINISHED BLOCK SIZE: 12˝

Butterflies go where they will, even to settle in quiet repose upon courthouse steps. Dilly-dallying and dawdling the day away, they lounge in flirtatious array without a care in the world. This project, a two-color twist on the traditional Courthouse Steps block, is a variation of the Log Cabin block. For those of you with more colorful tastes, a scrap basket of light and dark fabrics may also hold the promise of inspiration for this project.

Fabric Requirements:

- ▷ Butterfly Background: 1 yard
- ▷ Butterflies: ¼ yard
- ▷ Light Steps: 2 ½ yards
- ▷ Dark Steps: 3 ½ yards
- ▷ Inner Border: 2 ½ yards or ½ yard
- ▷ Outer border: 2 ½ yards
- ▷ Backing: 9 ¾ yards
- ▷ Binding: ¾ yard

Cutting Instructions:

Butterfly Block

Backgrounds

- ▷ 168 – 2″ light print squares

Butterflies

- ▷ 84 – 1 ¼″ scrap print squares

Courthouse Block

- ▷ 84 – 2″ x 3 ½″ light print rectangles (A)
- ▷ 84 – 2″ x 6 ½″ light print rectangles (C)
- ▷ 84 – 2″ x 9 ½″ light print rectangles (E)
- ▷ 84 – 2″ x 6 ½″ dark print rectangles (B)
- ▷ 84 – 2″ x 9 ½″ dark print rectangles (D)
- ▷ 84 – 2″ x 12 ½″ dark print rectangles (F)

Label the strips A, B, etc., as you cut them.

Inner Border

- ▷ 2 – 1 ¾″ x 84 ½″ dark print strips
- ▷ 2 – 1 ¾″ x 75″ dark print strips

Or

- ▷ 9 – 1 ¾″ dark print strips from width of fabric

Outer Border

- ▷ 2 – 7 ½″ x 87″ medium print strips
- ▷ 2 – 7 ½″ x 89″ medium print strips

Binding

▷ 10 – 2 ¼″ dark print strips from width of fabric

Butterfly Block

1. To make a wing unit, fold a 1 ¼″ butterfly print square in half diagonally, wrong sides together. Gently press on the fold. Place the folded square in the corner of a 2″ background square.

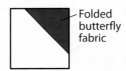
Folded butterfly fabric

2. Lay another 2″ background square on top, right sides together, making a sandwich. Sew along an edge, as shown in the diagram below. Stitch seams carefully, being sure to keep raw edges and corners of the fabrics aligned. Make two wing units.

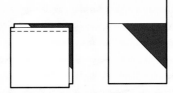

3. Flip the "wings" of the wing units so they go in opposite directions when the units are put right sides together. Sew. Press the seams open or break the seam and press them in opposite directions. Make 42.

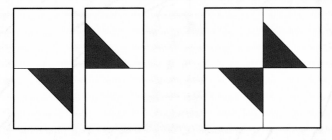

Courthouse Block

1. Paying close attention to the orientation of the butterfly block, as shown below, sew two 2″ x 3 ½″ light print A rectangles to opposite sides of the unit made in step 3. Press the seams to the light rectangles.

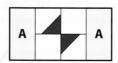

2. Sew two 2″ x 6 ½″ dark print B rectangles to opposite sides of the unit made in step 1. Press the seams toward the dark rectangles. Size the block to measure 6 ½″ square.

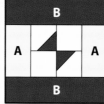

3. Sew two 2″ x 6 ½″ light print C rectangles to opposite sides of the unit made in step 2. Press the seams toward the light rectangles.

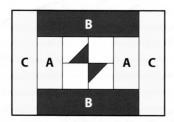

4. Sew two 2″ x 9 ½″ dark print D rectangles to opposite sides of the unit made in step 3. Press the seams toward the dark rectangles. Size the block to measure 9 ½″ square.

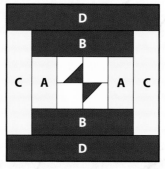

5. Sew two 2″ x 9 ½″ light print E rectangles to opposite sides of the unit made in

step 4. Press the seams toward the light rectangles.

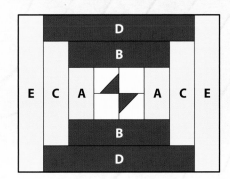

6. Sew two 2″ x 12 ½″ dark print F rectangles to opposite sides of the unit made in step 5. Press the seams toward the dark rectangles. Size the block to 12 ½″ square. Make 42 Courthouse blocks.

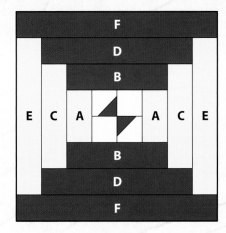

7. Assemble the blocks in rows according to the quilt diagram on page 48.

Borders

1. Using the 1 ¾″ x 84″ border strips, sew one to each long side of the quilt top. Press the seams toward the dark print border.

2. Using the 1 ¾″ x 75″ border strips, sew one to the top and bottom of the quilt top. Press the seams toward the dark print border.

3. Using the 7 ½″ x 87″ border strips, sew one to each side of the quilt top. Press the seams toward the medium print border.

4. Using the 7 ½″ x 89″ border strips, sew one to the top and bottom of the quilt top. Press the seams toward the medium print border.

5. Quilt and bind.

"The green grass and the happy skies court the fluttering butterflies." — Terri Guillemets

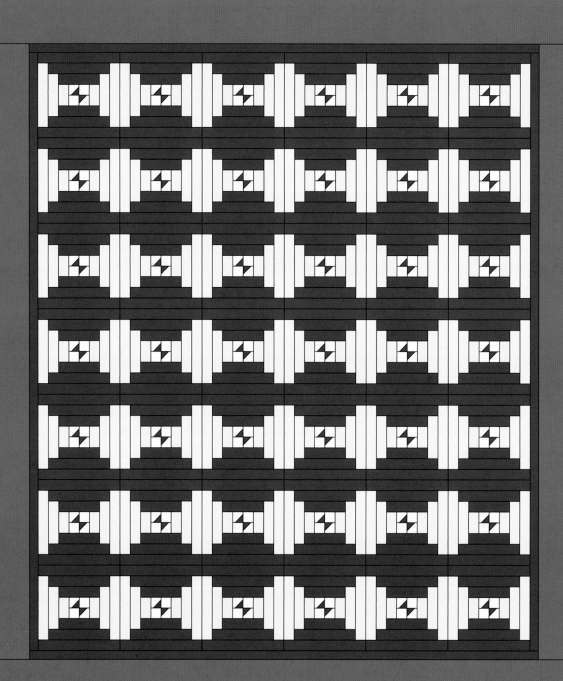

Butterfly Goes A-Courtin' Layout Guide

Garden Invitation

The Wild Indigo Duskywings *Erynnis baptisiae*
April to October

Butterfly Nectar

Goldenrod, Blue-Flowered Asters,
Swamp Milkweed & Pussytoes

Caterpillar Cuisine

Wild Indigo & Crown Vetch

Wild Indigo Duskywings
Photo by Betsy Betros

Butterfly Garden

PIECED BY: BETSEY LANGFORD

QUILTED BY: LINDSAY LAWING

Early morning moments spent in the garden can be times of quiet and peaceful contentment. One imagines Lady Sun smiling as she stretches forth fingertips, lovingly dancing across a pastel sea of flower petals and leaving behind her sunrise glow. Betsey's blending of soft shades of green and peach in Butterfly Garden are reminiscent of such a morning sunrise, a time of peaceful waiting and expectation. Delight in the simple block design of this quilt. Use Betsey's delicate, whispery shades of color or choose your own garden hues.

Fabric Requirements

Fabric	Throw 49 Blocks 68˝ Square	Twin 63 Blocks 64˝ x 84˝	Full 81 blocks 84˝ Square	Queen 100 Blocks 92˝ Square
Butterflies (peach print)	⅓ yard	½ yard	⅝ yard	⅝ yard
Yellow prints	1 ¼ yards	1 ⅝ yards	2 yards	2 ½ yards
Light green prints	1 ¼ yards	1 ⅝ yards	2 yards	2 ½ yards
Green print	1 ¼ yards	1 ⅝ yards	2 yards	2 ½ yards
Outer Border (green print)	2 yards	2 ½ yards	2 ½ yards	3 yards
Inner Border (peach print)	⅓ yard	⅓ yard	½ yard	½ yard
Binding (peach print)	½ yard	⅔ yard	⅔ yard	¾ yard
Backing	4 ½ yards	5 ½ yards	8 ¼ yards	9 yards

Note: For the blocks we used different prints totaling the yardage needed to create a scrappier look. We used three different yellows and two different light greens.

Cutting Instructions

Note: cutting instructions will allow for making 2 extra blocks. This gives you the freedom to substitute per your preference of color or placement.

Throw Quilt

Butterfly blocks

▷ 68 – 2 ½˝ yellow print background squares
▷ 68 – 2 ½˝ light green print background squares
▷ 68 – 2 ½˝ green print background squares
▷ 102 – 2 ⅛˝ peach print butterfly squares

Garden blocks, cut:

▷ 17 – 4 ½˝ yellow print squares
▷ 17 – 4 ½˝ x 8 ½˝ yellow print rectangles
▷ 17 – 4 ½˝ light green print squares
▷ 17 – 4 ½˝ x 8 ½˝ light green print rectangles
▷ 17 – 4 ½˝ green print squares

▷ 17 – 4 ½″ x 8 ½″ green print rectangles

Inner Border, cut:

▷ 6 – 1 ½″ x width of fabric (WOF) peach print strips

Outer Border, cut:

▷ 2 – 5 ½″ x 58 ½″ green print strips
▷ 2 – 5 ½″ x 68 ½″ green print strips

Binding, cut:

▷ 7 – 2 ¼″ x WOF peach print strips

Twin Quilt

Butterfly blocks

▷ 84 – 2 ½″ yellow print background squares
▷ 84 – 2 ½″ light green print background squares
▷ 84 – 2 ½″ green print background squares
▷ 126 – 2 ⅛″ peach print butterfly squares

Garden blocks

▷ 21 – 4 ½″ yellow print squares
▷ 21 – 4 ½″ x 8 ½″ yellow print rectangles
▷ 21 – 4 ½″ light green print squares
▷ 21 – 4 ½″ x 8 ½″ light green print rectangles
▷ 21 – 4 ½″ green print squares
▷ 21 – 4 ½″ x 8 ½″ green print rectangles

Inner Border

▷ 7 – 1 ½″ x WOF peach print strips

Outer Border

▷ 2 – 5 ½″ x 74 ½″ green print strips
▷ 2 – 5 ½″ x 68 ½″ green print strips

Binding

▷ 8 – 2 ¼″ x WOF peach print strips

Full Quilt

Butterfly Blocks

▷ 108 – 2 ½″ yellow print background squares
▷ 108 – 2 ½″ light green print background squares
▷ 108 – 2 ½″ green print background squares
▷ 162 – 2 ⅛″ peach print butterfly squares

Garden Blocks

- ▷ 27 – 4 ½″ yellow print squares
- ▷ 27 – 4 ½″ x 8 ½″ yellow print rectangles
- ▷ 27 – 4 ½″ light green print squares
- ▷ 27 – 4 ½″ x 8 ½″ light green print rectangles
- ▷ 27 – 4 ½″ green print squares
- ▷ 27 – 4 ½″ x 8 ½″ green print rectangles

Inner Border

- ▷ 8 – 1 ½″ x WOF peach print strips

Outer Border

- ▷ 2 – 5 ½″ x 74 ½″ green print strips
- ▷ 2 – 5 ½″ x 84 ½″ green print strips

Binding

- ▷ 9 – 2 ¼″ x WOF peach print strips

Queen Quilt

Butterfly blocks

- ▷ 136 – 2 ½″ yellow print background squares
- ▷ 136 – 2 ½″ light green print background squares
- ▷ 136 – 2 ½″ green print background squares
- ▷ 204 – 2 ⅛″ peach print butterfly squares

Garden blocks

- ▷ 34 – 4 ½″ yellow print squares
- ▷ 34 – 4 ½″ x 8 ½″ yellow print rectangles
- ▷ 34 – 4 ½″ light green print squares
- ▷ 34 – 4 ½″ x 8 ½″ light green print rectangles
- ▷ 34 – 4 ½″ green print squares
- ▷ 34 – 4 ½″ x 8 ½″ green print rectangles

Inner Border

- ▷ 9 – 1 ½″ x WOF peach print strips

Outer Border

- ▷ 2 – 5 ½″ x 82 ½″ green print strips
- ▷ 2 – 5 ½″ x 92 ½″ green print strips

Binding

- ▷ 10 – 2 ¼″ x WOF peach print strips

Butterfly Block

1. To make a wing unit, fold a 2 ⅛″ peach print butterfly square in half diagonally, wrong sides together. Gently press on the fold. Place the folded square in the corner of a 2 ½″ background square.

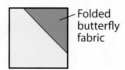

Folded
butterfly
fabric

2. Lay another 2 ½″ background square on top, right sides together, making a sandwich. Sew along a side with the butterfly fabric. Stitch seams carefully, being sure to keep raw edges and corners of the fabrics aligned. Make two wing units.

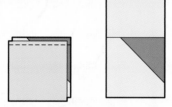

3. Flip the "wings" of the wing units so they go in opposite directions when the units are put right sides together. Sew. Press the seams open or break the seam and press them in opposite directions. Size the butterfly block to 4 ½″ square.

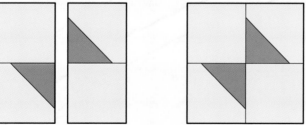

4. Referring to the Fabric Requirements chart, make the total number butterfly blocks required, using different background fabrics (yellow, light green or green) for a nice variety.

Garden Blocks

1. Sew a butterfly block to a 4 ½″ yellow, light green or green print square. Note that the butterfly blocks can be turned any direction.

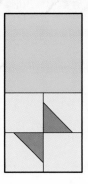

2. Sew the unit created in the previous step to a 4 ½″ x 8 ½″ print rectangle. Press the seams toward the rectangle. Size the block to 8 ½″ square.

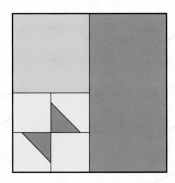

3. Repeat using different print rectangles and squares. Refer to the photo on page 59.

Quilt Assembly

1. Sew the Butterfly Garden blocks together into rows, randomly turning the blocks.

2. Sew the rows together as illustrated in the assembly diagram.

3. Sew an Inner Border piece to each side, and then sew an Inner Border piece to the top and bottom.

4. Repeat these same steps for the Outer Border sides, top and bottom.

5. Quilt as desired, being careful to not catch the edges of the butterflies.

6. Bind and enjoy.

"The butterfly counts not months but moments and has time enough." — Rabindranath Tagore

Painted Lady, photo by Patrick di Natale

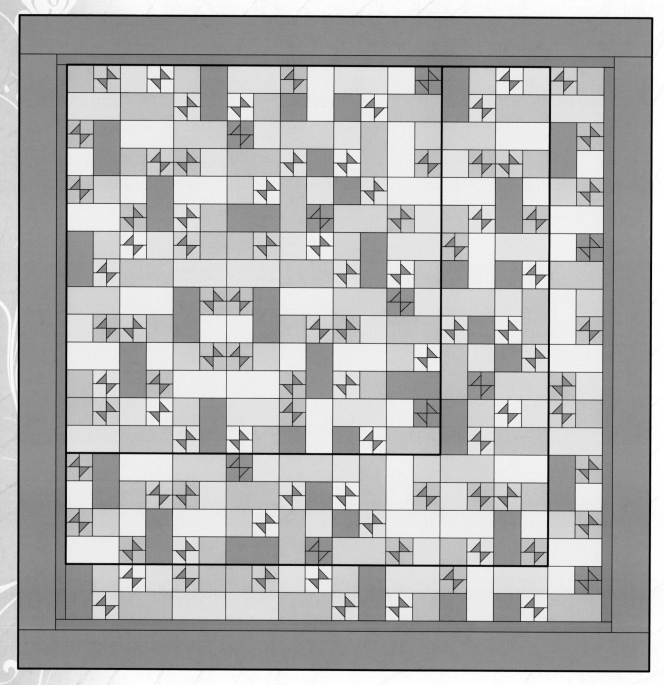

Butterfly Garden Layout Guide

Bronze Copper
Photo by Betsy Betros

Garden Invitation

The Bronze Copper *Lycaena hyllus*
February to November

Butterfly Nectar

Sharp-Toothed Mountain Mint & Swamp Milkweed

Caterpillar Cuisine

Dock Leaves & Knotweeds

Butterfly Towels

Why not bring that whimsical garden mood indoors? That is exactly what Betsey was thinking as she considered what to do with some leftover blocks from the Butterfly Garden Throw. Why not turn them into something beautiful and useful? With the extra blocks, rickrack, and pre-purchased hand towels, she created this pair of adorable kitchen towels. Bring a ray of sunshine to your own kitchen with this quick, easy project.

Fabric Requirements

▷ *Butterfly Block Background: 3″ x 5″ yellow print scraps, one scrap darker than the other
▷ *Butterflies: 1 – Fat Eighth or 1 – 2″ x 12″ scrap of light print
▷ Borders: ⅛ yard or 1 – 1 ¼″ x width of fabric (WOF) green print
▷ Tabs: 1 Fat Eighth or 1 – 6″ x 9″ yellow print
▷ Rickrack: 1 ⅛ yards (1″ wide rickrack works best)
▷ 1 Purchased kitchen towel, about 18″ wide

Or 3 leftover butterfly blocks from the Butterfly Garden Throw

Cutting Instructions:

Butterfly Block:

▷ 12 – 2 ½″ x 2 ½″ background print squares
▷ 6 – 2″ x 2″ butterfly squares

Borders:

▷ 2 – 1 ¼″ x width of fabric green print strips

Side Tabs:

▷ 2 – 4 ½″ x 6″ yellow print rectangles

Sewing Instructions

Butterfly Block

1. To make a wing unit, fold a 2″ butterfly square in half diagonally, wrong sides together. Finger press the fold. Place the folded square in the corner of a 2 ½″ x 2 ½″ background print square, as shown in the diagram.

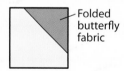

Folded butterfly fabric

2. Lay another 2 ½″ background print square on top, right sides together, making a sandwich. Sew along one edge as shown in the diagram. Stitch seams carefully, being sure to keep raw edges and corners of the fabrics aligned. Make two wing units.

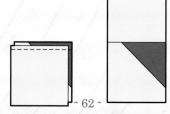

3. Flip the "wings" of the wing units so they go in opposite directions when the units are placed right sides together. Sew. Press the seams open or break the seam and press them in opposite directions. Make 3 Butterfly blocks.

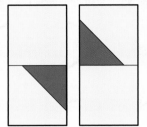 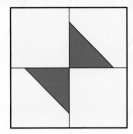

Quilt Assembly:

1. Sew the three Butterfly blocks together in a row.

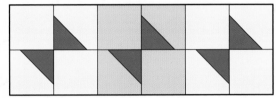

2. Sew one tab to each end of the strip of Butterfly blocks.

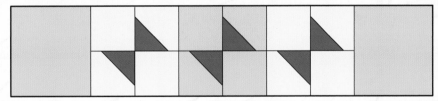

3. Trim the tabs equally to measure 1″ longer than the width of the towel.

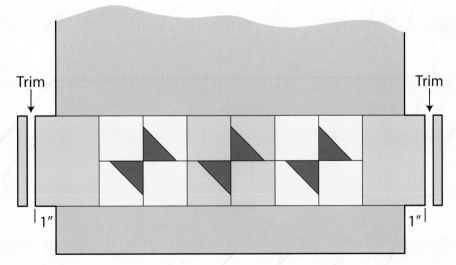

~ 63 ~

4. Sew a border strip to the top and bottom of the butterfly strip.

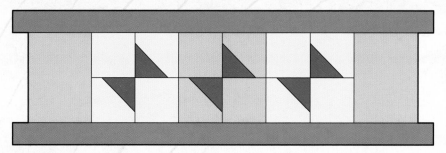

5. Trim the ends of the borders to match the tabs.

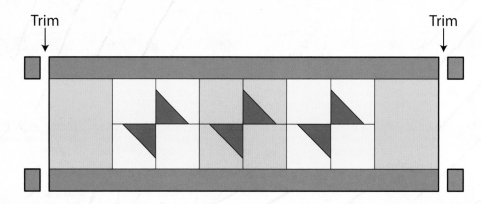

6. Press the top and bottom edges of the borders under ¼″ to create a finished edge.

7. Trim the rickrack to match the length of the butterfly strip.

8. Pin the rickrack to the reverse side of the butterfly strip, allowing half of the rickrack to show beyond the edge.

9. Pin the butterfly strip into place 2″ from the bottom edge, matching the center of the middle butterfly block with the center of the towel.

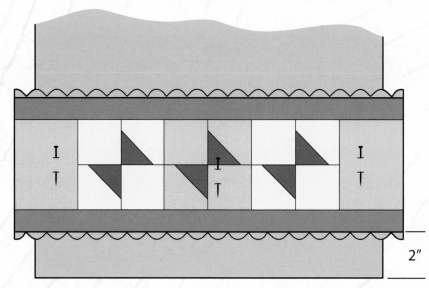

10. Topstitch along the edge of the borders, securing the rickrack and the butterfly strip to the towel all in one step.

11. Press the ends of the strip that fold around the edge of the towel under ¼" to create finished edges.

12. Whipstitch the ends of the strip to the reverse side of the towel.

"Just living is not enough," said the butterfly, "one must have sunshine, freedom and a little flower." — Hans Christian Andersen

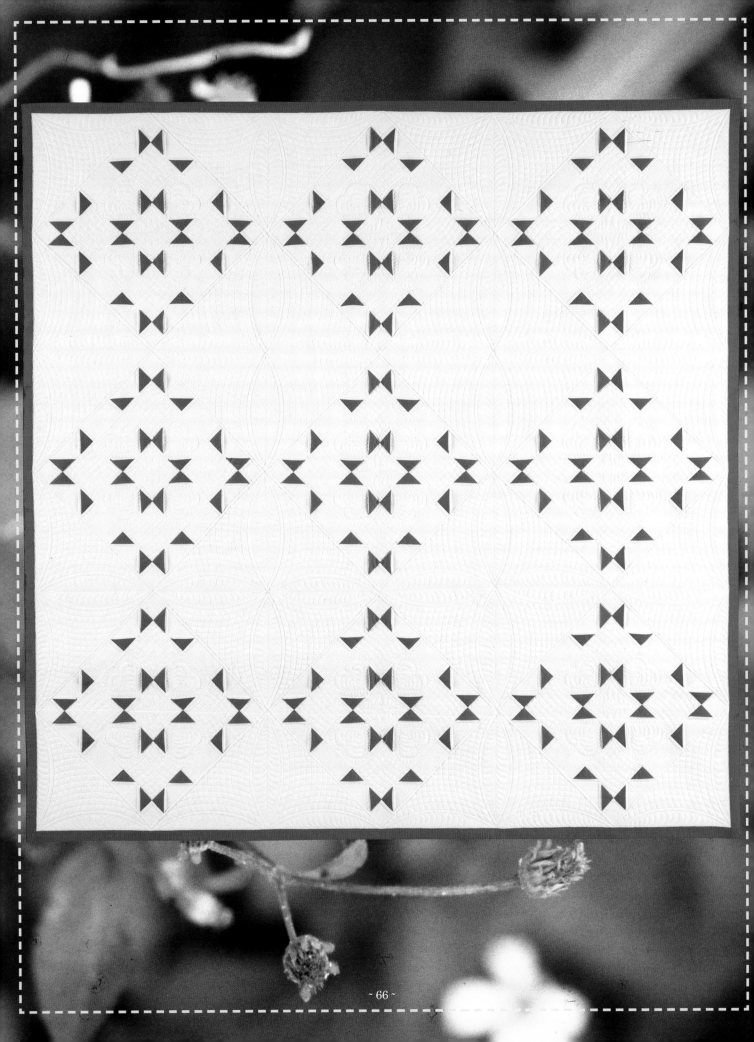

Garden Invitation

The Zebra Swallowtail *Eurytides marcllus*
March to October

Butterfly Nectar
Lantana & White Dutch Clover

Caterpillar Cuisine
Pawpaw Trees

Zebra Swallowtail
Photo by Betsy Betros

Butterfly Star

PIECED BY BETSEY LANGFORD
QUILTED BY LISA SIPES
FINISHED SIZE: 70˝ X 70˝
FINISHED BLOCK SIZE: 16˝

Traditional white is the perfect background canvas for a host of red butterflies. The butterflies float in airy spaces of each individual star block. Combined, they dance across the fabric like celestial fairies, a magnificent array of winged creatures capturing the simple elegance of two-color quilting.

Fabric Requirements

- ▷ Butterfly Points and Binding: 2 yards of solid red fabric
- ▷ Star Block Background and Setting Blocks: 6 yards of solid white fabric
- ▷ Backing: 8 ½ yards

Cutting Instructions

Butterfly Star Blocks

- ▷ 216 – 2 ⅛″ x 2 ⅛″ solid red squares
- ▷ 360 – 2 ½″ x 2 ½″ solid white squares
- ▷ 36 – 2 ½″ x 4 ½″ solid white rectangles
- ▷ 36 – 2 ½″ x 8 ½″ solid white rectangles

Setting Block

- ▷ 4 – 16 ½″ x 16 ½″ solid white squares

Setting Triangles

- ▷ 2 – 23 ⅞″ x 23 ⅞″ solid white squares; cut in half twice diagonally to make 8 side setting triangles. Cut the setting triangles using this method to avoid having bias on the outside of the quilt top.

Corner Triangles

- ▷ 2 – 12 ⅜″ solid white squares; cut in half once diagonally

Border

- ▷ 8 – 1 ½″ x width of fabric solid red strips

Binding

- ▷ 8 – 2 ¼″ x width of fabric solid red strips

The Butterfly Star Block

1. To make a wing unit, fold a 2 ⅛″ red square in half diagonally, wrong sides together. Gently press on the fold. Place the folded square in the corner of a 2 ½″ white square.

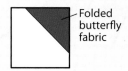

2. Lay another 2 ½″ white square on top, right sides together, making a sandwich. Sew along one edge as shown in the diagram below. Stitch seams carefully, being sure to keep raw edges and corners of the fabrics aligned. Make two wing units.

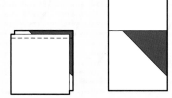

3. Flip the "wings" of the wing units so they go in opposite directions when placed right sides together. Sew. Press the seams open or break the seam and press them in opposite directions. Make 8 butterfly blocks.

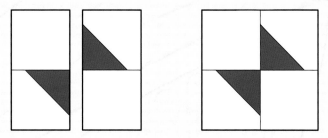

4. Sew four of the butterfly units together to form the center of the Butterfly Star block, as illustrated below.

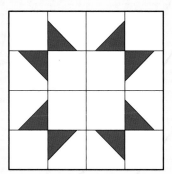

5. Fold a 2 ⅛″ accent print square in half diagonally wrong sides together. Gently press on the fold. Place the folded square in the corner of a 2 ½″ light print square.

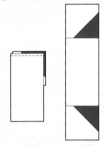
Folded butterfly fabric

6. Lay a 2 ½″ x 4 ½″ light print rectangle on top of the unit created in step 5, right sides together, making a sandwich. Sew along one short end, as shown in the diagram below. Stitch the seam carefully, being sure to keep raw edges and corners of the fabrics aligned. Repeat for the other end of the light print rectangle, matching the direction of the wing as shown below. Press the seams toward the light print rectangle. Make 4.

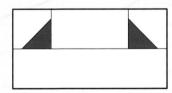

7. Sew a unit created in step 6 to a 2 ½″ x 8 ½″ white rectangle. Make 4.

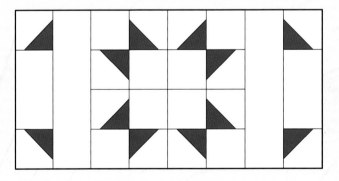

8. Sew two units made in Step 7 to a 2 ½″ x 8 ½″ white rectangle. Make 4.

9. Sew a butterfly unit to each end of the remaining units created in step 7.

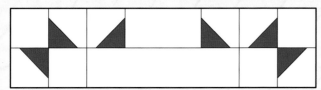

10. Sew the units created in step 9 to the top and bottom of the block, as shown in the block assembly diagram.

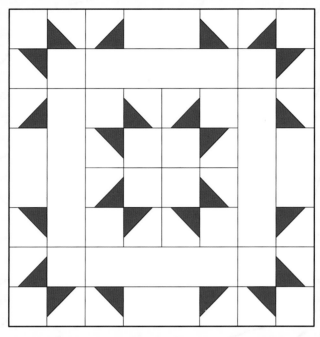

Quilt Assembly

1. Sew the Butterfly Star Blocks to an alternate block to make on-point rows. Add the setting triangles to each end. See the assembly diagram for placement.

2. Sew the rows together.

3. Sew two 1 ½″ x WOF solid red strips together and trim to 68 ½″. Sew a 1 ½″ x 68 ½″ solid red strip to each side of the quilt center.

4. Sew two 1 ½″ x WOF solid red strips together and trim to 70 ½″. Sew a 1 ½″ x 70 ½″ solid red strip to the top and bottom of the quilt center.

5. Quilt as desired and bind.

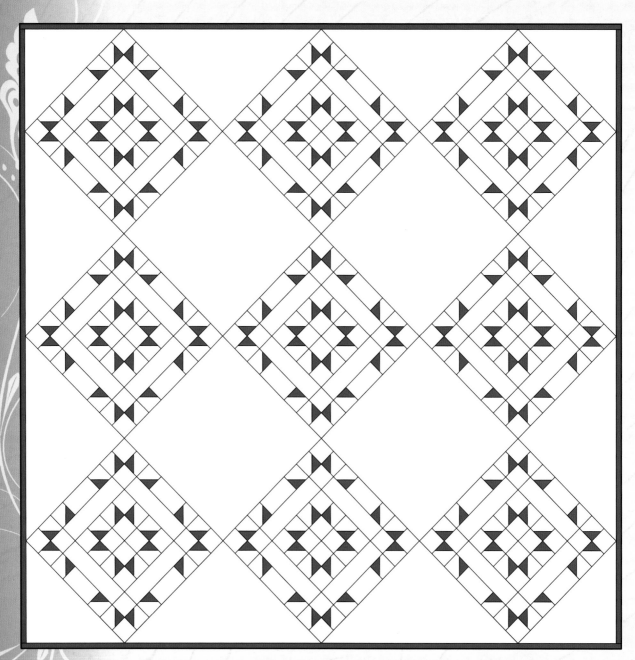

Butterfly Star Layout Guide

"Flowers and butterflies drift in color,
illuminating spring." — Author Unknown

Gulf Fritillary, photo by
Patrick di Natale

Little Glasswing Skipper
Photo by Betsy Betros

Garden Invitation

The Little Glasswing Skipper *Pompeius verna*
May to early August

Butterfly Nectar

Purple Coneflower & Gay Feather

Caterpillar Cuisine

Purpletop Prairie Grass

Framed Butterfly Star

BLOCK SIZE: 16″ X 16″

Quilts can show up in the most amazing places, including frames. The elegance of two-color contrast is a perfect way to showcase your creative quilting talents. Start with two fabrics you love, one for the butterfly field and one for the butterflies. Stitch your vision into reality. Choose the perfect frame for your handiwork and lovingly display it for all to see and admire.

Fabric and Supplies

▷ Butterflies: 1 Fat Quarter accent print fabric
▷ Background: ⅝ yard light print fabric
▷ Purchased or recycled frame with appropriate size opening
▷ Mat board to fit frame

Cutting Instructions:

▷ 24 – 2 ⅛″ x 2 ⅛″ accent (butterfly) print squares
▷ 40 – 2 ½″ x 2 ½″ light print squares
▷ 4 – 2 ½″ x 4 ½″ light print rectangles
▷ 4 – 2 ½″ x 8 ½″ light print rectangles
▷ 2 – 2 ½″ x 16 ½″ light print rectangles
▷ 2 – 2 ½″ x 20 ½″ light print rectangles

The Butterfly Star Block

Following steps 1 – 10 on pages 69-71 to create one Butterfly Star Block.

11. Sew a 2 ½″ x 16 ½″ light print rectangle to each side of the butterfly star block.

12. Sew a 2 ½″ x 20 ½″ light print rectangle to the top and bottom of the butterfly star block.

13. Press.

14. Mount the block on mat board, securing the edges on the back with archival tape.

15. Fit into the frame but do not use glass so that the 3-dimensional butterflies can fly freely.

Note: To use an odd size or premade frame adjust the borders to fit the frame.

Enjoy!

"Moss covered paths between scarlet peonies,
Pale jade mountains fill your rustic windows.
I envy you, drunk with flowers,
Butterflies swirling in your dreams."
— Ch'ien Ch'i, translated by Kenneth Rexroth

Zebra Longwings, photo by Patrick di Natale

Garden Invitation

The Cabbage White *Pieris rapae*
February to November

Butterfly Nectar

Mountain Mint, Hillside Chrysanthemum & Dandelions

Caterpillar Cuisine

Cabbage, Kale, Broccoli & Sweet Rocket

Cabbage White (Right)
Photo by Betsy Betros

Butterfly Comes to Dinner

PIECED BY CAROLYN NIXON
QUILTED BY BARBARA STEPHENS

*W*ith 3-D butterflies on the brain, Betsey and Carolyn sat down to dinner. A little conversation and *voilà*, there came a thought! Why not a Butterfly Comes to Dinner tablecloth? With a flick of Betsey's pen, there magically appeared a lovely table covering in two sizes. Carolyn quickly gave life to the design by gathering fabric and stitching up this rose-filled garden of butterflies. This project is fit to adorn any table, large or small. Impress that special loved one by serving a candlelight dinner on a table draped with your own version of this butterfly-adorned tablecloth.

Fabric Requirements

Fabric	Small Tablecloth 16 Blocks 60″ x 60″	Large Tablecloth 60 blocks 79″ x 79″
Background (main print)	3 yards	4 ¾ yards
Butterfly and Accent	½ yard	1 yard
Butterfly Background	¾ yard	2 ¼ yards
Backing	4 yards	7 ½ yards
Binding	½ yard	⅔ yard

Cutting Instructions for Small Tablecloth

For the background, cut:

▷   1 – 17 ½″ light floral square
▷   2 – 14 ½″ x 31 ½″ light floral rectangles
▷   2 – 14 ½″ x 59 ½″ light floral rectangles

For the Butterflies and Accent Borders, cut:

▷   32 – 1 ¾″ red tone-on-tone squares
▷   6 – 1″ red tone-on-tone strips from the width of the fabric
▷   2 – 1″ x 17 ½″ red tone-on-tone strips
▷   2 – 1″ x 18 ½″ red tone-on-tone strips
▷   2 – 1″ x 30 ½″ red tone-on-tone strips
▷   2 – 1″ x 31 ½″ red tone-on-tone strips

For the Butterfly background, cut:

▷   64 – 3 ½″ green tone-on-tone squares

For the Binding, cut:

▷   7 – 2 ½″ red tone-on-tone strips from the width of the fabric

Cutting Instructions for Large Tablecloth

For the background, cut:

▷ 1 - 17 1/½″ light floral square
▷ 2 - 14 ½″ x 31 ½″ light floral rectangles
▷ 2 - 14 ½″ x 60 ½″ light floral rectangles
▷ 2 - 4″ x 72 ½″ light floral strips
▷ 2 - 4″ x 79 ½″ light floral strips

For the Butterflies and Accent Borders, cut:

▷ 120 – 1 ¾″ red tone-on-tone squares
▷ 2 – 1″ x 17 ½″ red tone-on-tone strips
▷ 2 – 1″ x 18 ½″ red tone-on-tone strips
▷ 2 – 1″ x 30 ½″ red tone-on-tone strips
▷ 2 – 1″ x 31 ½″ red tone-on-tone strips
▷ 16 – 1″ red tone-on-tone strips from the width of the fabric

For the Butterfly Background, cut:

▷ 240 – 3 ½″ green tone-on-tone squares

For the Binding, cut:

▷ 9 – 2 ½″ red tone-on-tone strips from the width of the fabric binding

The Butterfly Block

1. Fold a 1 ¾″ red tone-on-tone square in half diagonally, wrong sides together. Gently press on the fold. Place the folded square in the corner of a 3 ½″ green tone-on-tone square.

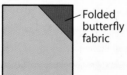

Folded
butterfly
fabric

2. Lay another 3 ½″ green tone-on-tone square on top, right sides together, making a sandwich. Sew along one edge as shown in the diagram. Stitch seams carefully, being sure to keep raw edges and corners of the fabrics aligned. Make two wing units.

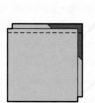

3. Flip the "wings" of the wing units so they go in opposite directions when placed right sides together. Sew. Press the seams open or break the seam and press them in opposite directions. Make 16 for the small tablecloth and 60 for the large tablecloth.

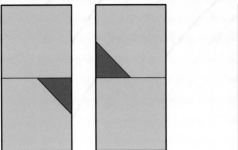 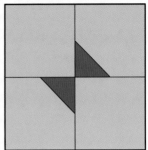

Tablecloth Assembly Instructions

Small Tablecloth

1. Sew a 1″ x 17 ½″ red tone-on-tone strip to the sides of the center 17 ½″ light floral square.

2. Sew a 1″ x 18 ½″ red tone-on-tone strip on the other sides of the center.

3. Sew 3 butterfly blocks together to make the next border. Make 2 sets.

4. Sew a unit created in the previous step to each side of the center.

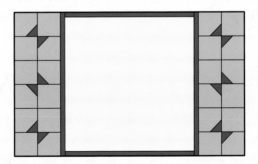

5. Sew 5 butterfly blocks together to make the next border. Make 2 sets.

6. Sew a unit created in the previous step to each side of the center according to the assembly diagram.

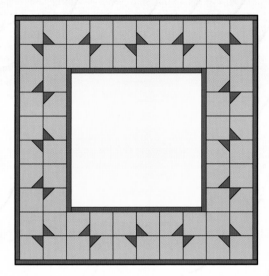

7. Sew a 1″ x 30 ½″ red tone-on-tone strip to each side of the center.

8. Sew a 1″ x 31 ½″ red tone-on-tone strip to the top and bottom of the center.

9. Sew a 14 ½″ x 31 ½″ light floral rectangle to each side of the center.

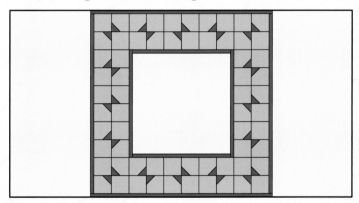

10. Sew a 14 ½″ x 59 ½″ light floral rectangle to the top and bottom of the center. Square up the tablecloth to 59 ½″ if needed.

11. Sew two 1″ x width of fabric red tone-on-tone strips together. Cut the strip to 59 ½″. Repeat to make two 1″ x 59 ½″ strips.

12. Sew a 1″ x 59 ½″ red tone-on-tone strip to each side of the center.

13. Sew two 1″ x WOF red tone-on-tone strips together. Cut the strip to 60 ½″. Repeat to make a total of two 1″ x 60 ½″ strips.

14. Sew a 1″ x 60 ½″ red tone-on-tone strip to the top and bottom of the center.

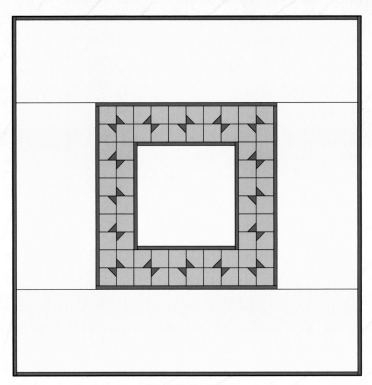

Small Tablecloth

Large Tablecloth

Follow steps 1 – 14 as for the small tablecloth to make the center.

15. Make 44 additional butterfly blocks as described in steps 1 - 3.

16. Sew 10 Butterfly blocks together, alternating directions of the butterflies. Make two sets.

17. Sew one set created in the previous step to each side of the center. Square to 72 ½" if needed.

18. Sew 12 butterfly blocks together alternating directions of the butterflies. Make 2 sets.

19. Sew a set created in the previous step to the top and bottom of the center. Square to 72 ½″ if necessary.

20. Sew two 1″ x WOF red tone-on-tone strips together. Cut the strip to 72 ½″. Repeat to make a total of two 1″ x 72 ½″ strips.

21. Sew a 1″ x 72 ½″ red tone-on-tone strip created in the previous step to each side of the center.

22. Sew two 1″ x WOF red tone-on-tone strips together. Cut the strip to 73 ½″. Repeat to make a total of two 1″ x 73 ½″ strips.

23. Sew a 1″ x 73 ½″ red tone-on-tone strip created in the previous step to the top and bottom of the tablecloth center.

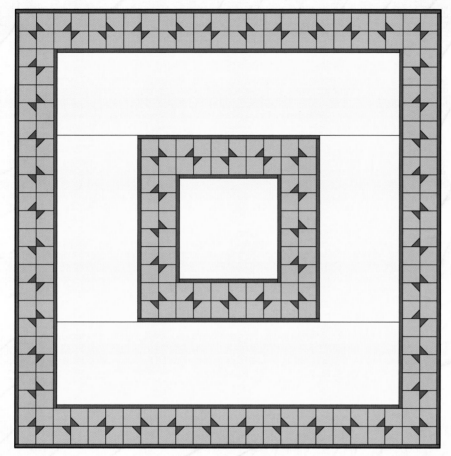

Large Tablecloth

24. Sew a 4" x 73 1/2" light floral strip to each side.

25. Sew a 4" x 80 1/2" light floral strip to the top and bottom.

Quilt and bind.

"Happiness is a butterfly, which when pursued, is always just beyond your grasp, but which, if you sit down quietly, may alight upon you." — Nathaniel Hawthorne

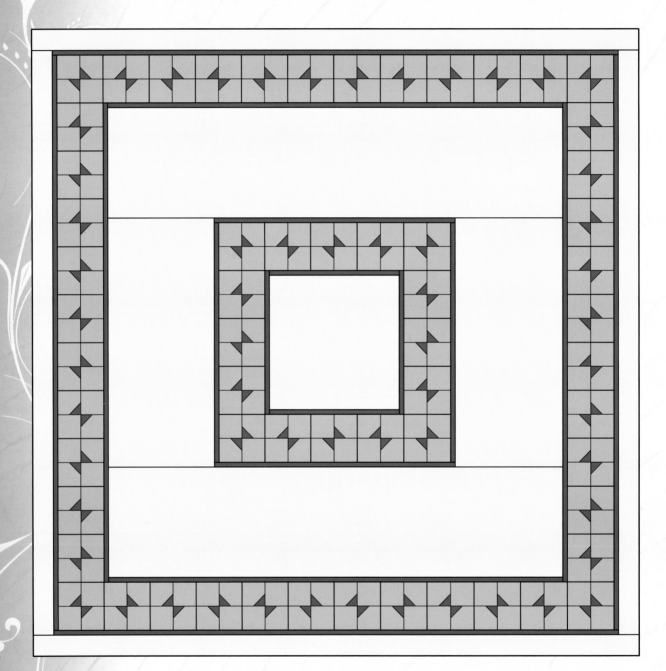

Butterfly Comes to Dinner Layout Guide

Eastern Tiger Swallowtail
Photo by Betsy Betros

Garden Invitation

The Eastern Swallowtail *Papilio glaucus*
March to October

Butterfly Nectar

Butterfly Bush, Sweet William & Zinnias

Caterpillar Cuisine

Spicebush, Magnolias, Wild Cherry Trees & Tulip Trees

Mama's Black Pearls

PIECED BY CAROLYN NIXON
QUILTED BY BARBARA STEPHENS

On the darkest of nights and the brightest of days, your echoes linger on the wind. From scraps of nothingness, you created things of beauty. I can do nothing greater than to follow your soft footsteps through time. Look at the blocks, Mama. See the black pearls and those nine-patch blocks you love. Most of all, my sweet mother, feast your eyes on the butterflies. I made them to remember you and the wings of life you gave to me.

~Carolyn Nixon (Journal Entry, 2002)

Fabric Requirements:

Fabric	Throw 70″ x 79″	Full 79″ x 88″	Queen 88″ x 97″
Dark Scraps	37 fat sixteenths or 2 ½ yards of assorted dark scraps	46 fat sixteenths or 3 yards of assorted dark scraps	56 fat sixteenths or 3 ½ yards of assorted dark scraps
Light Scraps	56 fat sixteenths or 3 ½ yards of assorted light scraps	71 fat sixteenths or 4 ½ yards of assorted light scraps	86 fat sixteenths or 5 ½ yards of assorted light scraps
Black	2 ½ yards	3 ¼ yards	4 yards
Binding (⅜″ double fold)	⅝ yard	¾ yard	¾ yard
Backing	4 ⅞ yards	7 ⅛ yards	7 ½ yards
* a fat sixteenth is a 9″ x 11″ piece of fabric			

Cutting Instructions:

Throw Quilt:

▷ 128 – 5″ solid black squares
▷ 1118 – 2″ light print scrap squares
▷ 733 – 2″ dark print scrap squares

Full Quilt:

▷ 162 – 5″ solid black squares
▷ 1402 – 2″ light print scrap squares
▷ 915 – 2″ dark print scrap squares

Queen Quilt:

▷ 200 – 5″ solid black squares
▷ 1718 – 2″ light print scrap squares
▷ 1117 – 2″ dark print scrap squares

Black Pearl Block Assembly

1. Draw a diagonal line on the reverse side of four 2″ light print squares.

2. Place a marked 2″ light print square in the bottom left corner of a 5″ solid black background square, right sides together, making sure the edges align.

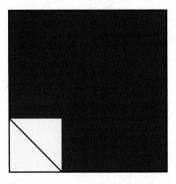

3. Sew on the line. Press the seam toward the black square.

4. Flip the 2″ light print square open to be sure it is even. If it is, trim seam to ¼″.

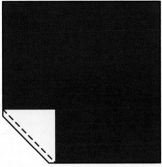

5. Repeat steps 2 through 4 on the remaining three corners to complete the Pearl Block. Make 128 Black Pearl blocks for the throw, 162 blocks for the full size and 200 blocks for the queen size.

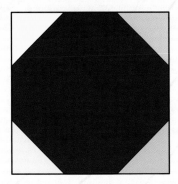

Nine-Patch Block

1. Sew a 2″ dark print square to both sides of a 2″ light print square to make the top row of the nine-patch block. Press the seams toward the dark print squares. Repeat to make a bottom row.

2. Sew a 2″ light print square to both sides of a 2″ dark print square to make the middle row of the nine-patch block. Press the seams toward the dark print square.

3. Sew the rows together as illustrated. Press the seams toward the top and bottom rows. Repeat steps 1 through 3 to make 127 nine-patch blocks for the throw, 161 blocks for the full size and 199 blocks for the queen size.

Quilt Assembly

1. Sew the Black Pearl blocks to a Nine Patch blocks to make rows. Alternate the placement of the blocks for odd and even rows (see diagram).

Odd Rows

Even Rows

2. Sew the rows together. For the throw, make 17 rows of 15 blocks. For the full size, make 19 rows of 17 blocks. For the queen size, make 21 rows of 19 blocks.

3. Sew a row of a variety of 2″ squares around the outside of the quilt for a border.

4. Quilt and bind.

"I do not know whether I was then a man dreaming I was a butterfly, or whether I am now a butterfly dreaming I am a man." — Chuang Tzu

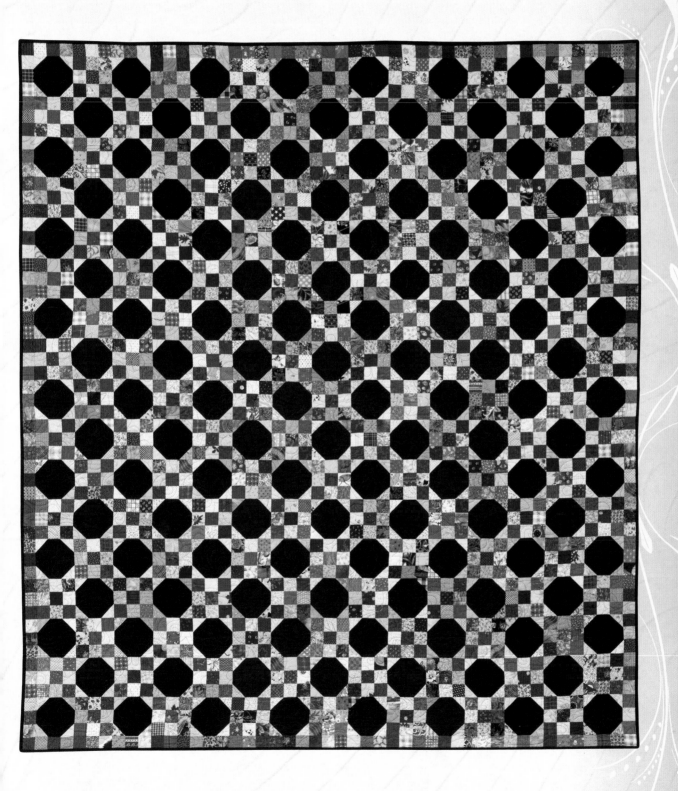

More Books from Kansas City Star Quilts

For a complete list or to order books, go to Pickledishstore.com

Or call StarInfo at (816) 234-4242.

Kansas City Star Quilts   www.PickleDish.com